The Twelve

A Bible Class Study Guide

by Josh Ketchum
www.JoshKetchum.com
Seven Oaks Church of Christ - Mayfield KY

Purpose and Aim:

1. This book is intended for classroom study and use by a teacher and students.
2. This book follows and relies heavily upon the book **Twelve Ordinary Men** by John MacArthur. One will get the most out of this workbook by reading MacArthur's book as well.
3. This book is not intended to complete the student's knowledge, but to inspire it and allow for further discoveries as a class, thus there will often be open-ended questions for discussion and reflection.

Seven Oaks Church of Christ
290 State Route 97
Mayfield KY 42066
270-247-5201
www.sevenoakschurchofchrist.com
www.JoshKetchum.com
jketchum@sevenoakschurchofchrist.com
josh@joshketchum.com

Copyright © 2013 by Josh Ketchum

All rights reserved.

ISBN-13: 978-1489533036
ISBN-10: 1489533036

1st Edition Printed May 2013

Cover Photo: The Exhortation to the Apostles by James Tissot
Public Domain Photo because of its age. Taken from:
http://commons.wikimedia.org/wiki/File:Brooklyn_Museum_-
_The_Exhortation_to_the_Apostles_(Recommandation_aux_apôtres)_
-_James_Tissot.jpg

Primary Version Used in this Work
English Standard Version

Table of Contents

Introducing the Apostles
Part 1

I. The extraordinary story of the apostles.

   A. "From our human perspective, the propagation of the gospel and founding of the church hinged entirely on twelve men whose most outstanding characteristic was their ordinariness." John MacArthur

   B. They did not come from the religious or educated elite of their day.

   C. They were given to many failings and shortcomings.

   D. Christianity has spread the world over thanks to their work.

II. The Time of their Training (MacArthur - p. 1-8)

   A. Jesus entire ministry from baptism to resurrection lasted about three years.

   B. The intensive training of the twelve lasted about half that long; 18 months.

   C. Jesus had grown extremely popular, though controversial in the larger Galilean region. (Luke 6:11-12, etc.) But instead of focusing on the multitude Jesus chose to concentrate on a few.

   D. The opposition to Jesus was peaking. They were planning how they might destroy him. So

Jesus began to focus on twelve men who he would depend upon to carry his work forward.

E. "Do for one what you can't do for all." Andy Stanley

F. How is Christ's strategy here different from our typical thinking?

III. The Titles of the Twelve

A. "Disciples" - *mathetes* in Greek - The word means "learners or students." It carries the idea of a pupil or one who follows the teaching of a teacher or master. It is a broad term throughout the gospels indicating those who followed Jesus. It is used of the Twelve in Matt. 10:1; 11:1; 12:1; Mark 8:27; Luke 8:9; John 2:2; 3:22,

B. "apostles" - *apostoloi* in Greek - The word means "messengers or sent ones." It means a delegate, specifically an ambassador for the gospel, a commissioner of Christ who is sent forth with orders. This term becomes a title and is used specifically for the Twelve. (Mat. 10:1-4, Luke 6:13, Acts 1:26, Rev. 21:14). The term occurs 79 times in the NT and of these 68 are in Luke and Paul. These men had authority in the church and revealed the doctrine and Word of God (Ephesians 4:11, 1 Cor. 12:28ff). Others who wanted to assume to this authority and position where called "false apostles" by

Paul in 2 Corinthians 11:5, 13). Paul was equal to these original twelve as one "born out of due time" (1 Cor. 15:8).

C. "The Twelve" - *dodeka* in Greek - The number is significant as they had to select Matthias to replace Judas (Acts 1). The gospel writers often will refer to the apostles with this designation. Matthew uses the term "apostles" only once (Mat. 10:2), but elsewhere uses "the twelve" (Mat. 11:1; 20:17). Mark likewise only uses the term "apostles" once (Mark 6:30), but speaks of "the twelve" often (Mark 3:14; 4:10; 6:7; 9:35; 10:32; 11:11; 14:10, 17, 20, 43). John also always refers to the group as "the twelve" (John 6:67, 70-71; 20:24)

IV. The Stages of their Work (MacArthur - ch. 1)

A. Call to Conversion
Early stages of John's gospel record this stage. This was them learning about Jesus and His message. We might think of this stage as them being converted to Christ. They look to him for salvation, yet they maintain their full-time jobs and live at home predominantly.

B. Call to Ministry

Luke 5:1-11 describes this event when they are called to be "fishers of men." Mat. 4:19-22 also describe this phase.

C. Call to the apostleship
This next stage is when they are selected from the broad number of disciples to the special office of an apostle.   This is recorded in Matthew 10:1-4 and Luke 6:12-16.   This work begins with them being sent out two by two for evangelistic work (Mark 6:7ff)

D. Call to Martyrdom
The last stage could be described as their call to give their lives for Christ. This is the stage of their preaching and teaching during the book of Acts and beyond.   History tells us that all give their lives in a martyr's death except John who died in exile as an old man. Paul described the work of the apostles in the eyes of the world in graphic terms (1 Cor. 4:9-13)

Introducing the Apostles
Part 2

I. They were common and ordinary men
   A. The twelve should not be elevated to a super-human level. They should be viewed like the rest of us as disciples of Jesus. His choice of ordinary men, speaks to the fact that he can use all kinds of people.
   B. Why would he choose the lowly, humble, and ordinary?
      1. His ministry and work were in direct conflict with the religious hierarchy and teachers of the day.
      2. To demonstrate their power comes from the message they preach and the man Jesus Christ.
      3. 1 Corinthians 1:20-21, 27-29, 2:5
   C. Yet, we also must not underestimate their example.
      1. They sought the Lord.
      2. They sacrificed greatly.
      3. They were "holy" in their lifestyle and character.

II. Jesus' Selection Process
   A. We examined their stages earlier in lesson one. For further study and clarification let me share A.B. Bruce's description and stage breakdown from the book - *The Training of the Twelve*

The twelve arrived at their final intimate relation to Jesus only by degrees, three stages in the history of their fellowship with Him being distinguishable. In the **first stage** they were simply believers in Him as the Christ, and His occasional companions at convenient, particularly festive, seasons. Of this earliest stage in the intercourse of the disciples with their Master we have some memorials in the four first chapters of John's Gospel, which tell how some of them first became acquainted with Jesus, and represent them as accompanying Him at a marriage in Cana, at a passover in Jerusalem, on a visit to the scene of the Baptist's ministry, and on the return journey through Samaria from the south to Galilee.

In the **second stage**, fellowship with Christ assumed the form of an uninterrupted attendance on His person, involving entire, or at least habitual abandonment of secular occupations. The present narratives bring under our view certain of the disciples entering on this second stage of discipleship. Of the four persons here named, we recognize three, Peter, Andrew, and John, as old acquaintances, who have already passed through the first stage of discipleship. One of them, James the brother of John, we meet with for the first time; a fact which suggests the remark, that in some cases the first and second stages may have been blended together—professions of faith in Jesus as the Christ being immediately followed by the renunciation of secular callings for the purpose of joining His company. Such cases, however, were probably exceptional and few.

The twelve entered on the **last and highest stage** of discipleship when they were chosen by their Master from the mass of His followers, and formed into a select band, to be trained for the great work of the apostleship. This important event probably did not take place till all the members of the apostolic circle had been for some time about the person of Jesus

B. The selection of the apostles - Luke 6:12-16
1. This is really a mysterious and amazing event.

       1. How did the human and divine sides of Christ work?
       2. This was prayer and communication with His Father.
   B. What was Christ praying for?
       1. Who He would choose?
       2. The men they He had decided to choose?
       3. His training of them?
       4. His plan of focusing on these twelve?
   C. Greek word is *dianuktereuo* - It speaks of enduring a task through the night. It has the sense of toiling through the night or staying at a task all night. He stayed awake all night and persevered. He could have prayed as many as 10 to 12 hours.

C. Why Twelve?
   A. Obviously twelve parallels the twelve tribes of Israel.
   B. What type of message was Jesus sending by selecting twelve apostles to lead his kingdom?
       A. It was a direct assault upon Judaism and the powerful religious hypocrites of his day. In some ways a message of judgment against Israel.
       B. Luke 22:29-30

Introducing the Apostles
Part 3

I. Their Role and Purpose
    A. Their role and purpose was truly great. This fictitious story illustrates:
When the angels welcomed Jesus home there was this conversation. "What is it all about? they asked Jesus. "The redemption of the world" answered the Lord. "But you have come back here," said the angels, "How will the world know of it?" "I have trained my men" replied Jesus. "To evangelize the world?" the angels asked. "Yes, indeed." the Savior replied. "Every corner of it." "How many men did you train for such a mammoth task?" "Twelve men" answered Jesus. "Just a handful! But what if they fail?" "If they fail," said Jesus, "I have no other plans." "But is that not a great risk to take?" "No." said the Lord, "because they will not fail." (The Twelve, p. 175)

    B. Their role was to be "fishers of men."
        1. The great commission was first given to them.
        2. Mat. 28:18-20, Mark 16:15-16, Luke 24:44-49
        3. They were to preach the gospel of Christ.

    C. They were to convey the teachings of Jesus.
        A. Acts 2:42
        B. Matthew 16:19
        C. Ephesians 2:20 - They served as the foundation of the church and

established the doctrines of Christ for the church.

D. They recorded the Word of God through inspiration of the Holy Spirit.

D. They were to be examples and leaders to the church.

    A. 1 Cor. 4:9-13

    B. As leaders of the church they were to be holy and consecrated to God. The church looked to them for their example. 1 Cor. 11:1

    C. They were to equip and edify the church.

        A. Ephesians 4:11-12

    D. They had great authority and power.

        A. Miraculous power to confirm the Word and their role.

        B. Authority in the church as leaders.

E. They were "sent out" ones with the full authority and message of the one who sent them; Jesus Christ. They were His delegates. They spoke with His authority, delivered His message, and were given His power.

    A. The first-century Jewish culture had *shaliah* which were official representatives of the Sanhedrin, or ruling council. They exercised the full rights of the Sanhedrin. They spoke for them and with their authority. Yet, they never delivered their own message, but the message of the group. They were sent out to deliver messages, settle disputes, and conduct business. Some prominent rabbis also had their *shaliah*. The apostles functioned in much the same way and were likely viewed in much the same light as Jesus' *shaliah* (MacArthur p. 20-21).

II. Their Weaknesses (p. 24-27 of MacArthur)
   A. They lacked spiritual understanding.
      1. They were at times thick, dull, blind, and slow to understand.
      2. So, Jesus just kept teaching.
   B. They lacked humility
      1. They were self-absorbed, self-centered, self-promoting, and proud (i.e. Mat. 20:20-28, Mark 9:33-37, Luke 9:46).
      2. So, Jesus became an example of humility modeling servant leadership to them.
   C. They lacked faith.
      1. Jesus rebuked them, "O you of little faith." (Matthew 6:30, 8:26, 14:31, 16:8).

  2. So, Jesus sought to increase their faith through doing miracles and constantly demonstrating His divinity.

 D. They lacked commitment.

  1. They all forsook him and fled at his arrest (Mark 14:50).

  2. So, Jesus prayed for them (John 17).

 E. They lacked power.

  1. On their own they were weak and helpless.

  2. So, Jesus empowered them with His Holy Spirit.

Why would Jesus pick men like this? "His strength is made perfect in weakness." 2 Cor. 12:9, Acts 4:13, Luke 6:40

How do we relate to their weaknesses?

Peter

(This is a long lesson, it may require more than one week.)

I. The Groupings of the Twelve. - MacArthur (p. 30)

Mat. 10:2-4	Mark 3:16-19	Luke 6:14-16	Acts 1:13
Peter Andrew James John	Peter James John Andrew	Peter Andrew James John	Peter James John Andrew
Philip Bartholomew Thomas Matthew	Philip Bartholomew Matthew Thomas	Philip Bartholomew Matthew Thomas	Philip Thomas Bartholomew Matthew
James (less) Lebbaeus Simon Judas Iscariot	James (less) Thaddeus Simon Judas Iscariot	James (less) Simon Judas Judas Iscariot	James (less) Simon Judas

A.   What lessons about group dynamics do we learn?

B.   What do we learn about intimate and close relationships?

   1.   How many can one individual maintain?

   2.   Was Jesus equally close to all twelve disciples?

II. The Calling of the Disciples with a focus on Peter.

A. Does the accounts of the calling of Peter, Andrew, James and John conflict?

Our answer is found by noticing the location of the events and piecing the accounts together. (*A map of Palestine during the time of Christ is helpful*)

John 1:35-51

John's account happened first. It is the beginning of Jesus'ministry. John the Baptist was baptizing "in Bethabara beyond the Jordon" (1:28). This is in the southern region near the Dead Sea. Andrew and Peter were disciples of John, from Bethsaida, a city on the Sea of Galilee (1:44). They were down south following John the Baptist. Jesus is baptized by John, tempted by the Devil, pronounced to be the "Lamb of God" by John the Baptist. This causes Andrew and an unnamed disciple to seek Jesus (1:37). They dwell with him for the night. Andrew, Peter, Philip, and Nathaniel apparently stay with Jesus on his trip to Cana of Galilee, where He proves his deity by turning water to wine (2:1-11). Then (2:12) they go down to Capernaum which is a city on the Sea of Galilee.

Mat. 4:18-22, Mk. 1:16-20, and Luke 5:1-11

This is when the scene can be shifted to the Synoptic Gospels (Mat., Mk, Lk). They speak of Jesus teaching in Capernaum and other cities around the Sea of Galilee called by Luke the "Sea of Gennesaret" (Lk 5:1). Apparently the disciples had gone back to fishing at least for a short time. This makes sense, since they were from this region. Jesus seeing and knowing them calls them to be fishers of men. He is teaching them a powerful lesson through a miracle (Lk 5) about how they will do great things through Him.

Read Mat. 4:18-22, Mk. 1:16-20, and Luke 5:1-11 and notice their surrounding context. It does seem that they know one another, especially in Luke's account in ch. 5. The geography and the time table lines up correctly.

III. Getting into the Text:

    A. John 1:25-42
        1. What was it like growing up a child during this time period? What hopes and convictions were the Jewish parents passing on to their children?
        2. These men were looking for the Messiah. They were disciples of John.
        3. We first should want to share Jesus with our family. (1:40)
        4. Jesus immediately gives Simon a nickname.
Simon - "He has heard" - Symbol of vacillating, shifting, and unsteady ways. It also is a way of referring to his old life. Jesus will use this name when Simon is on the wrong course; when he is wavering.
Peter - *Petros* - Greek - *Cephas* - Aramaic. Symbol for what Jesus wanted him to become. He was to be that rock of a leader. He was to be firm, faithful, and strong.

　　　　5.　In many ways, Peter's two names come to represent the two sides of his and our faith.

B.　Matthew 4:18-22
　　　1. Jesus invites them to follow Him as He goes on a preaching tour throughout Galilee.
　　　2. Jesus intention was to make them "fishers of men."

C. Luke 5:1-11
　　　1. Jesus teaches them that He is the master over everything. They think they know fishing better than Him, but He can empower them to do it better.　He is teaching them their need for dependence upon Him and what is possible through their service.
　　　2. Peter, though resistant, did obey.
　　　3. Why does Peter fall down and say, "Depart from me, for I am a sinful man" (v. 8)?
　　　　a. Why is this important for his service?
　　　　b. How is this story a pattern for the beginning place for all followers of Christ?

IV. Some Key Events of Peter's Life

　　A.　Matthew 14:22-36
　　　1. Why did Peter get out of the boat?
　　　2. What does this say about his personality?
　　　3. Why did he sink?
　　　4. What lessons can we learn from Peter here?

B. Matthew 16:13-28
1. How had God revealed this knowledge to Peter?
2. What is the "rock" that Jesus is referring to in verse 18?
3. What is Jesus giving to Peter and the rest of the apostles later when he speaks of the "keys to the kingdom"?
4. (v. 22) - Why did you think Peter felt the need to rebuke Jesus?
    a. Was Peter worried about Jesus or Peter?
    b. Did he understand the gospel fully yet?
5. How does Jesus' teachings in v. 24-28 apply to the lesson Peter needed to learn in v. 23?

C. Arrest and Trials of Jesus
1. Peter's **Confidence**
Luke 22:31-34
Matthew 26:30-35
2. Peter's **Apathy**
Matthew 26:36-46
3. Peter's **Foolish Courage**
John 18:6-11
4. Peter's **Denials**
John 18:15-18, 25-27
Matthew 26:69-75
Luke 22:54-62
5. Peter's **Reaction**
Luke 22:62

D. The Restoration of Peter to Jesus - John 21:5-19
   1. What is Jesus trying to accomplish in this conversation?
   2. What lessons for our own failures should we learn from this text?

E. Day of Pentecost and Early Preaching - Acts 2
   1. What did Peter accomplish as a person in preaching that day?
   2. What did he have to overcome to preach on Pentecost?
   3. Acts 5:27-32
      a. What changes does this indicate in Peter from the earlier man who denied Jesus?
      b. What is his sole aim and priority in life?

F. Peter and the Gentiles
   1. The story of the conversion of Cornelius and his household.
      a. Acts 10-11
      b. Why is this so significant?
      c. What must it have required of Peter?
      d. What was he risking in being involved in such a revolutionary act of accepting the Gentiles into Christ?
   B. Peter's prejudice in Galatia
      a. Galatians 2:11-14
      b. What was Peter doing sinful?
      c. How do you think Peter handled this sin?

d. Acts 15:7-14 - Peter learned and took a stand to correct other Christians and lead the church in the right path.

Peter wrote 1 and 2 Peter. Strong tradition teaches us that he was crucified upside down along with his wife.

What are some overall lessons we should draw from his life?

V. Three key elements that go into making a true leader (Outline from ch. 2 of MacArthur)

   A. The raw material that makes a true leader.
      1. Inquisitiveness
      2. Initiative
      3. Involvement
   B. The life experiences that shape a true leader.
      1. Glorious experiences like viewing the miracles, seeing the transfiguration, and being with Jesus.
      2. Difficult experiences like being rebuked by Jesus, denying the Lord, and showing prejudices.
      3. Peter learned so many lessons from his experiences, it is hard to read his epistles without reflecting on how Peter himself had learned the lesson he is teaching.
   C. The character qualities that define a true leader.

1. Lasting leadership is grounded in character. It is a necessary quality of spiritual leadership.
2. Peter demonstrated and learned:
   a. Submission (1 Peter 2:13-18)
   b. Restraint (1 Peter 2:21-23)
   c. Humility (1 Peter 5:5-6)
   d. Love (1 Peter 4:8
   e. Compassion (1 Peter 5:8-10)
   f. Courage (1 Peter 1:3-7)

We are blessed by studying Peter because he challenges us to be so much more than we are, yet, we identify with his frailties and failings. In every Christian there is a little bit of Simon and a little bit of Peter. We need to seek to be like him and put one to death, while ever growing and developing the rock of faith within us.

"But grow in the grace and knowledge of our Lord and Savior Jesus Christ. To him be the glory both now and to the day of eternity. Amen."
(2 Peter 3:18 ESV)

Andrew

Andrew was a member of the leading four-some of apostles. He is the most inconspicuous member of the group. He is not included in several of the main events where we see the closer circle of Peter, James, and John (Mat. 17:1, Mark 5:37, 14:33). He is included with them on two occasions (Mark 1:29, 13:3).

It is helpful to review our previous discussion regarding the calling of Peter, Andrew, James and John as disciples. They meet Jesus when traveling with John the Baptist in John 1. They later are called to a higher level of discipleship by Jesus in Matthew 4:18-22 and Luke 5:1-11.

Andrew's name appears 13 times in the New Testament. All of these are in the gospels except Acts 1:13. Four of these involve his name appearing in the list of the 12 apostles. The nine other times involve Andrew being mention in the midst of gospel accounts.

I. Somethings to Ponder

A. There is nothing negative said in Scripture about Andrew as an individual. He would be guilty of failings as a group of apostles like their lack of faith, misunderstandings, arguments over greatness, and being scattered during the arrest and trials. But anytime Andrew is mentioned it is doing something either in word or deed right. He is not mentioned very often, but when he is mentioned it is good.

    1. Contrast this with Peter: Which one would you rather be if the Holy Spirit was going to record your life?

    2. What might this say about his personality compared to Peter?

B. Andrew's relationship to Peter is an interesting one to study. "In such situations, where one brother overshadows another to such a degree, it is common to find resentment, strong rivalry, or even estrangement" (MacArthur p. 63). Yet, in Andrew's case there is no evidence of hard feelings. We all know situations where a younger or older brother/sister had trouble because of the fame, personality, or success of another sibling.

    1. John 1:35-42

        a. They were serious religious men who were away from their work following John for this time.

        b. He was blessed to be able to spend much time with Jesus in fellowship.

        c. His first thought and desire was to find his brother Peter. They had both been looking for the Messiah and were excited about His coming. Andrew didn't want to keep this news to himself. Though Andrew is becoming one of the initial disciples of the Messiah, he doesn't want to leave Peter out, even though he likely knows Peter will be more dominant and attain leadership above him.

2. Throughout the accounts of Andrew, he appears the least contentious and most thoughtful of the four-some.   He is kind, approachable, and faithful.   The other three often appear brash, hasty, and impulsive.   Yet, they tend to get more glory and notoriety.   How do we handle it when our family members or a close friend takes precedence over us?

3. We might assume that Peter and Andrew were close, though different.   Scripture speaks of them owning a house together (Mark 1:29).   Tradition suggests they worked together extensively after Pentecost in evangelistic work.

C. Andrew's name means "manly."   It is a Greek name, which is somewhat surprising.   Andrew was no doubt a manly man in that he was a fisherman and spent time in the wilderness with John.

II. Some Lessons to Learn
     (Here are three lessons taken from MacArthur regarding Andrew.)

A. He saw the value of individual people.

1. Peter brought crowds to Jesus, but Andrew brought individuals to Jesus. In fact, it was Andrew who brought an individual, Peter, to Jesus.
2. Story of Jesus feeding the five thousand illustrates this point. John 6:1-14
    a. When the others were perplexed at Jesus' test for them to provide food, when they had no seeming way.
    b. Andrew found a young boy and brought his sack lunch to Jesus. John 6:8-9.
3. Story of the greeks coming illustrates this point. John 12:20-22
    a. Philip turned to Andrew to introduce them to Jesus.
    b. MacArthur called him the first home missionary (he brought his brother) and the first foreign missionary (he brought these greeks).
4. The most important and valuable aspect of evangelism is typically individual-to-individual.
    a. Most people are converted through the influence of some individual. We need to see the value in befriending one person and converting them to Christ. Or we may just need to consider our present friends and seek to convert them to Christ.

b. Observe these four points made by Chris Altrock on his blog about personal evangelism:

1) First, *involve* yourself in activities, events and habits which deepen your relationship with Jesus. It's true that people must be able to see the gospel in you as they hear the gospel from you. It's true that you need to experience the Good News so you can share the Good News. So, involve yourself in things that deepen your own relationship with Jesus.

2) Second, *invest* in loving relationships with people who may be far from God. Rarely is the gospel received when is shared from a distance. The context of genuine friendship and gracious hospitality provides evangelism the most fertile soil. The goal is to share not only Jesus but your very life as well. Every Christian should do this—not just paid staff. Every Christian needs to invest in loving relationships with non Christians.

3) With that foundation in place, *invite* that new friend to participate with you in things that introduce him/her to Christ and Christianity. This could be an invitation to attend a practical marriage seminar or a thriving small group. This is something every Christian can do.

4) Finally, *inform* your friend about Jesus. Verbalize the good news in ways that are meaningful and relevant. Often, we've made two mistakes when it comes to speaking about Jesus. First, we've tried to inform without investing. Ideally, speaking comes as part of this larger process. Second, we've focused on informing people about everything but Jesus. Don't merely inform that

friend about the church or talk to that friend about baptism. The first step is to inform him/her about Jesus. The gospel is first and foremost an announcement about Jesus. Use spoken words to share Jesus. (ChrisAltrock.com; 9-10-2012)

B. He saw the value in insignificant gifts.
1. In the feeding of the five thousand account, Andrew is the only apostle who sees the potential in such a meager gift of five loaves and two fish. He could have been embarrassed to even suggest such, but he had the faith and courage to take the boy to Jesus.
2. Andrew understood that no gift is insignificant in the Lord's hands.
3. Later in Luke 21:1-4, Jesus will teach them regarding the widow's two mites, that God's ability to use a gift is in no way hindered or enhanced by the size of the gift. The true measure of the gift's significance is the faithfulness of the giver, not the size.

C. He saw the value of inconspicuous service.
1. We get the since from Andrew that he was not interested in who got the credit, but in the job getting done. Christ needs more folks in His kingdom who are concerned about the greater good of Christ, rather than their personal role and position. The Bible cautions of desiring prominence as a teacher (James 3:1).

a. Jesus spoke to this in Mark 9:35.
b. Jesus exemplified this when he took a towel and washed his disciples feet.
c. Andrew was a model of service leadership and working behind the scenes to make a tremendous impact.

Tradition tells us that Andrew went to Scythia and Greece. It reports that he was crucified in Achaia, Greece after spending two days on the cross.

James, the Son of Zebedee

James was a common name in the gospels with three men being named James. This often causes some confusion for Bible students today. This breakdown of each man should help.

A. James, *the son of Zebedee* and brother of John
    A. This James is the focus of our study in this lesson.
    B. He was an apostle and was martyred by Herod Antipas in A.D. 44 (Acts 12:1-3)
B. James, *the son of Alphaeus* or James the Less
    A. This James will be studied later as he was an apostle, though little is known about him.
C. James, *the Lord's half-brother.*
    A. This James was a prominent leader in the early church in Jerusalem. Paul refers to meeting with him in Gal. 1:19, 2:9-12. He speaks during the Jerusalem council of Acts 15 involving the issue of circumcision.
    B. He is the author of the New Testament book of James and son to Joseph and Mary.

James, the Son of Zebedee

James is a part of the inner circle that was with Jesus in some of the most significant events. This group included Peter, James, and John. For example these three were with Jesus at the raising of Jarius' daughter (Mark 5:37), on the Mount of Transfiguration

(Mat. 17:1-8), and were with him in the garden of Gethsemene (Mat. 26:36-46).

James was the son of Zebedee (Mat. 4:21, 10:2; Mark 1:19; 3:17), and his wife Salome (Mat. 27:56; Mark 15:40). He was the elder brother to the apostle John (Mat. 17:1; Mark 3:17, 5:37; Acts 12:2). He was one of the earliest disciples of Jesus (Mat. 4:21-22).

Zebedee was likely a wealthy and influential man. This is hinted at by the fact that they are often referred to as "the sons of Zebedee." This might have stemmed from his financial success or his family lineage. His fishing business involved hiring multiple servants (Mark 1:20). His family had enough status and recognition that they were known by the High Priest in Jerusalem (John 18:15-16). Salome, his mother, is going to travel with Jesus and the apostolic band at times providing logistic support and financial support (Mat. 27:55, Mark 16:1, Luke 8:1-3).

This family prominence might have helped created the personality of James who is shown to be passionate, ambitious, self-confident, and outspoken. One might have expected him to have a greater leadership role within the apostles given his name, place, and prominence, but he is never mentioned in the gospels by himself, but always with his brother or the other apostles. His only single reference in the Bible comes in Acts 12 when his death is recorded.

I. The "Sons of Thunder" - Luke 9:51-56
   A. The nickname "sons of Thunder"
      1. This name is only recorded as being given to them in Mark 3:17. Like Peter's nickname, it was given as a description of personality traits.
      2. What type of traits would this nickname indicate?
   B. Jesus, going against typical Jewish practice, went directly through Samaria, instead of taking the longer way around Samaria in order to avoid contact with the "despised" Samaritans.
   C. The Samaritans didn't like Jews either, and felt like Jews were worshipping wrongly by going to Jerusalem for the Passover. So when Jesus and his group need lodging as they were traveling to Jerusalem for Passover, they are refused a place to stay.
   D. This apparently angered James and John which prompted them to ask the Lord if he wanted them to bring fire down upon the Samaritans to consume them.
   E. Understanding the Old Testament story recorded in 2 Kings 1 is essential for grasping why James and John suggested such an action.
      1. A key difference in the Elijah story is that he was being used as an

instrument of God's judgment. The motive was not personal or selfish in nature, but regarded a divine message of God. Also, likely Elijah's life and work was at stake had he been captured.

   2. The events of Elijah's day happened in this same region that the apostles were now traveling through.

F. But what were the motives and thoughts behind James and John's question? Luke 9:51-56

   1. What is implied with their question in terms of who would bring down the fire?

   2. How did Jesus answer their question and how did he handle the rejection?

G. Jesus mission was very different from Elijah's mission. Jesus came to save, not to destroy. Luke 9:55-56 (KJV, NKJV, NASV) (Also Luke 19:10, Mat. 20:28, John 3:17, John 12:46-47) Jesus will return a second time for judgment (2 Thess. 1:7-9).

H. How is it easy for us to have a "sons of Thunder" attitude? (1 Peter 2:21-25)

I. It is likely that many of these Samaritans later heard the gospel and came to salvation (Acts 8:5-8)

II. Thrones in the Kingdom - Matthew 20:20-24

A. A comparison of Mark's account (Mark 10:35-41) makes it clear that Salome was put up to this by James and John.
B. This request might have been hatched by Jesus' teaching in Mat. 19:28 regarding thrones. The brothers must have not heard the "many who are first will be last and the last first" (Mat. 19:30).
C. They were already in the intimate circle, but they wanted more.
D. They reply that they "are able" to drink the cup that I am to drink. What does this show us about the brothers?
E. How do you understand Jesus statement to them in Mat. 20:23?
F. This attitude of selfish-ambition caused the disciples to continue to argue about greatness. It is the subject of Jesus teaching in Mat. 20:25-28 and ultimately his teaching through washing their feet in the upper room (John 13).
    1. How were their attitudes wrong? How do these attitudes affect our relationships?
    2. How can our personal ambition be dangerous as a Christian?
    3. What did they not understand about the teachings and work of Jesus?
G. MacArthur has an insightful paragraph: "James wanted a crown of glory; Jesus gave him a cup of suffering. He wanted power;

Jesus gave him servanthood. He wanted a place of prominence; Jesus gave him a martyr's grave. He wanted to rule; Jesus gave him a sword--not to wield, but to be the instrument of his own execution. Fourteen years after this, James would become the first of the Twelve to be killed for his faith." (p. 91).

H. What type of man did James become? We know no details of his work after the resurrection besides the work of all of the apostles on Pentecost and in Jerusalem. But it seems that James remained a man of great passion. He is likely the first apostle to be martyred and the only one recorded in Scripture (Acts 12:1-3).

John, the Son of Zebedee

John is familiar to us because he wrote so much of the New Testament. He was the son of Zebedee and brother to James, the apostle who was put to death by Herod Agrippa I. We assume that his mother was Salome (Mat. 27:56, Mark 15:40). (See James for information regarding his family.)

John is one of the earliest disciples and is chosen to be an apostle (Mat. 4:21-22). His surname was Boanerges, that is Sons of Thunder, which Jesus gave to James and John evidently because of their temperament (Mark 3:17). He was a fisherman by trade. He grew up in the Galilee area.

He is going to be the author of the Gospel of John, 1, 2, and 3rd John, and Revelation. John played a major role in the early church. He was a member of the Lord's inner circle. He is a frequent partner with Peter in Acts 1 - 12. Yet, we rarely see him acting alone in the gospels. What was said of James' personality and character is also true of John. They are basically inseparable in the gospel accounts.

He will do a prominent work in the region of Asia minor and the city of Ephesus. He will be exiled to the isle of Patmos where he wrote Revelation. He is thought to have died a natural death in Ephesus in his 90s close to the turn of the century.

I. The "Sons of Thunder" and Desiring a Throne Review
   A. We studied this in the last lesson, so we will not do an extensive review.
   B. Sons of Thunder - Luke 9:51-56
      1. The brothers demonstrated their intolerant, judgmental attitude. They were zealous and aggressive in a bad way.
      2. The problem was their attitude. They were sectarian, narrow-minded, and impetuous.
   C. Desiring a Throne - Matthew 20:20-24
      1. They put their mother up to asking Jesus for them to have the best seats in His kingdom.
      2. This shows their selfish-ambition and desire for greatness. They did not understand the way of Jesus.

II. Taking Responsibility for Mary - John 19:26-27
   A. What do you think this story says about Jesus and John's relationship?
   B. "Several witnesses in early church history record that John never left Jerusalem and never left the care of Mary until she died" (MacArthur p. 115).

III. Lessons from John (MacArthur ch. 5)

A. The Theme of Love
  1. He is known as the apostle of love as its theme flows through his books. He used the word more than 80 times in his writings.
  2. This is a quality he learned through Christ. We can learn much about true love from a study of his writings.
  3. He is an amazing example of how Christ should transform and shape us.
  4. Contrary to what might be thought of today, his love for others did not cause him to compromise doctrine and truth.
  5. He is one of the most clear writers in Scripture. He sees things in black and white.

B. The Balance between Love and Truth
  1. John had a passion for truth as well as love.
  2. He used the term: 25 times in the gospel and 20 in the Epistles.
  3. Notice how John taught truth:
     a. John 8:31-32, 3 John 3-4
     b. He taught against error - 1 John 4:1-6
  4. Incident in Mark 9:38-41
     a. John is guilty of an unloving spirit because the man was not officially a member of the group.

b. Possibly John was confessing this to Christ because he was convicted by Jesus' teaching about being a servant rather than seeking greatness for self.

c. The kingdom needs men who have zeal, courage, ambition, and drive, but all of these must be balanced with love.

5. "Zeal for the truth must be balanced with love for people. Truth without love has no decency; it's just brutality. On the other hand, love without truth has no character; it's just hypocrisy (p. 106)."

6. Which direction do you think most tend to lean today?

a. The godly person must seek to cultivate both virtues and passions. Eph. 4:15

b. 2 John is a good example of how John balanced love and truth in dealing with false teachers.

III. The Balance between Ambition and Humility

1. In his youth, John was ambitious. "Ambition without humility becomes egotism or even megalomania (p. 108)."

2. John had asked for the best thrones (Mark 10:35-37).

a. "The error was in desiring to obtain the position more than they desired to be worthy of such a position. Their ambition was untempered by humility (p. 109)." See Mark 10:42-45

b. Jesus taught humility. Luke 18:8-14

c. He emphasized the truth that if you want to be great, you must become a servant of all.

3. John did eventually learn humility and it comes through in his writings.

a. John in the gospel refuses to speak of himself in reference to Jesus. He uses each reference to himself as a way of honoring Christ. He was the "disciple whom Jesus loved" (John 13:23; 20:2; 21:7, 20).

b. John will record the teaching of Jesus washing the disciples feet.

IV. The Balance between Suffering and Glory

A. In his earlier years he had a desire for glory and an aversion to suffering. All the disciples forsook Jesus and fled on the night of his arrest.

B. Mark 10:38-39

1. Though he did not give his life as a martyr, think of the suffering John endured.
2. HIs brother James was killed, He was exiled, He saw Christians persecuted.
C. He learned to look beyond his earthly sufferings to his eternal glory. Revelation 19-22

John, a man of ambition and intolerance, became a humble, gentle, loving man.   He was fiercely dedicated to truth and doctrinal purity. He still serves as a model for Christians today.

A traditional story of John says that late in his life when he was feeble. He would still visit churches and would deliver a short sermon, "My little children, Love one another."

Philip

Philip is the fifth apostle in all four lists of the twelve apostles. We might assume that he was the leader of the second group of four apostles. His name is a Greek name, and we are not given his Jewish name if he had one. His name means "lover of horses." He is paired in Matthew's gospel with Bartholomew, who is presumed to be his partner when they went out two-by-two (Mat. 10:3).

We should distinguish him from the evangelist and deacon of the early church also named Philip who lead the Ethiopian eunuch to Christ (Acts 6:5, 8:5-40). From the first three gospels all we learn about Philip is that he is one of the twelve. It is in the fourth gospel of John that we learn some more details of Philip.

Philip was from "Bethsaida, the city of Andrew and Peter (John 1:44)." He likely grew up with Andrew, Peter, James, and John. Many believe he was a fisherman by trade because of his association with the above fishermen and his returning to fishing after the resurrection in John 21. It is likely that Philip and Andrew were the unnamed "two others" of John 21:2 as they are often in the company of the men mentioned.

MacArthur views Philip as the following type of person:

"Piecing together all that the apostle John records about him, it seems Philip was a classic 'process person.' He was a facts-and-figures guy--a by-the-book, practical-minded, non-forward-thinking type of individual. He was the kind who tends to be a corporate killjoy, pessimistic, narrowly focused, sometimes missing the big picture, often obsessed with identifying reasons things can't be done rather than finding ways to do them. He was predisposed to be a pragmatist and a cynic--and sometimes a defeatist--rather than a visionary." (p. 121)

We wish to examine the Biblical text for ourselves and draw our own conclusions. While there is much merit to MacArthur's perspective, it seems to be a bit critical of Philip when considering the small amount of information we have about him.

I. His Call and Missionary Service - John 1:43-51
    A. Finding the Messiah - John 1:43-45
        1. We can assume that Philip was with Peter, Andrew, and John in the wilderness with John the Baptist (1:28-42).
        2. When Jesus was ready to return to Galilee he invited Philip to follow him as well as a disciple.
        3. Philip had been seeking the Messiah (1:45). They were looking for the coming King and Messiah. This is what had prompted them to follow John and his preaching ministry. Now Philip is overjoyed at having found Jesus.
    B. Bringing Nathanael to Christ - John 1:45-51

1. Like Andrew who went and found his brother, Philip went and found his friend Nathanael. Our friendships should provide fertile soil for evangelism.
2. Nathanael was skeptical. Bethsaida was slightly north of Nazareth and both were in Galilee. Nathanael came from Cana (John 21:2) which is also a village north of Nazareth. It seems there was some local rivalry reflected in his comments.
3. Philip replied with an answer we should give to the skepticism of our friends, "Come and see." We should encourage our friends to not take our word about Jesus, but to investigate Christ, His Word, and His salvation for themselves.

II. The Feeding of the Five Thousand - John 6:1-14
   A. This was a great multitude as the number 5,000 only reflects the number of men present.
   B. Jesus turns to Philip and asks him, "Where are we to buy bread, so that these people may eat?" (6:5). Jesus did this to test him.
   C. MacArthur suggests that Philip was the apostolic administrator. He was the one in charge of arranging the meals and logistics. Judas was in charge of keeping the money (John 13:29), so it would make sense to have one in charge of these matters. This may not have been an official position, but more just the role he played because of his personality.

D. Philip may have already of considered this problem. He responds that "two hundred denarii worth of bread would not be enough for each of them to get a little" (6:7).

1.Instead of thinking what an opportunity, he was thinking about the problem. He was looking with physical glasses, rather than through spiritual ones.

2. He was pessimistic. Some might just say realistic. Yet, he had seen the numerous works of Jesus and his possibilities. He had seen the water turned to wine, but he was still counting heads, dollars, and loaves.

E. Philip needed to think with a vision. He needed to have greater faith. Andrew comes through with a vision and greater faith. He takes a meager gift and gives it to Jesus trusting he can multiply his offering.

F. MacArthur writes, "Everything seemed impossible to him. He needed to set aside his materialistic, pragmatic, common-sense concerns and learn to lay hold of the supernatural potential of faith" (127).

III. The Visit of the Greeks - John 12:20-22

A. For whatever reasons these Greeks who were either God-fearing Gentiles or full-fledged proselytes to Judaism were coming to the Passover. They had obviously heard of Jesus and desired to meet him. For whatever reason

they take their request to Philip.   Maybe they heard he was the organizer of the group.
B. Maybe Philip really didn't know what to do about this issue, because rather than take them to Jesus himself, he tells Andrew.   Philip and Andrew then both introduce these Greeks to Jesus.
   1. Maybe it was because of Jesus' primary mission of going to the house of Israel that Philip was a bit unsure.
   2. See Mat. 10:5-6; 15:24.   But this principle was not meant to prohibit Gentiles from meeting Jesus, but rather just the priority of the ministry (Rom. 2:10, John 1:11-12).

IV. His Lack of Understanding in the Upper Room - John 14:8
A. This was the night of Jesus' betrayal and arrest. His time of teaching his disciples had come to an end.   He was trying to give them some final words of encouragement and strength.
   1. He had washed their feet (John 13), predicted his betrayer,   instituted the Lord's supper, and is now giving some instruction.
   2. Read the words of Jesus in John 14:1-7
B. Consider the statement of Philip (14:8) to the ears of Jesus.
   1. Jesus responded strongly with explaining that Philip had been looking at the Father this entire time (14:9-11).

2. Jesus is claiming His own deity and explaining the purpose of his work.
3. For Jesus it was an issue of Philip's faith (14:10).
C. How could Philip say such a statement?
   1. MacArthur writes, "For three years Philip had gazed into the very face of God, and it still was not clear to him. His earthbound thinking, his materialism, his skepticism, his obsession with mundane details, his preoccupation with business details, and his small-mindedness had shut him off from a full apprehension of whose presence he had enjoyed" (p. 133).
   2. W.E. Skipper wrote, "It was a devout and sincere wish for a disciple of Jesus to want to see the Father. The answer of Jesus was not a refusal, but a reminder to Philip that one who has seen Christ has seen God" (p. 24).
   3. What do you think? Do you agree with the critical assessment by MacArthur?

The last Philip is mentioned is in Acts 1:13 where he is in the upper room with the other disciples waiting for Pentecost.

The rest of his life is clouded in legend and mystery. By most accounts, and fairly good authority, he is put to death by stoning at Heliopolis in Phyrygia (Asia Minor) eight years after the martyrdom of James.

W.E. Skipper summarized his life: "He possessed an inquiring spirit, he was a practical straight forward man of common sense, he grew in faith and loyalty as he associated with Christ" (p. 24).

Like the other disciples, Philip is an example of God using weak, frail humans to accomplish His great work (1 Cor. 1:27-29).

Nathanael

It is often supposed that Nathanael is called Bartholomew in the four lists of the apostles (Mat. 10:3, Mark 3:18, Luke 6:14, Acts 1:13). It is believed that Nathanael is his proper name which means "God has given." His surname was Bartholomew. It is a Hebrew surname and means "son of Tolmai." This was common to be connected with one's father.

He is connected with Philip in three gospel lists and with Matthew in the list in Acts 1:13. The synoptic gospels and Acts tell us nothing about him, except that he is an apostle. The information we have regarding him involves him discovering Jesus through the influence of Philip. It might reasonably be supposed that they were close friends. Likely growing up together and working together as apostles. They both were from Galilee and made a pair like Peter and Andrew and James and John, though they were not fleshly brothers. Nathanael's home was in Cana of Galilee and he and Philip had likely come to hear the preaching of John the Baptist together.

Some reasons why we believe Nathanael and Bartholomew are the same individual (W.E. Skipper).
A. John who twice mentions Nathanael (John 1:45-51, 21:2) but does not speak of anyone whom he calls Bartholomew.

B. John tells us that Philip brought him to Jesus. The other gospel writers connect Philip with Bartholomew.

C. In John 1, the men who meet Jesus and become his disciples are John, Andrew, Peter, Philip, and Nathanael. The other men are prominent and known apostles. Nathanael is described as "an Israelite without guile" and as one who will "see heaven opened, and the angels of God ascending and descending on the Son of Man." This certainly seems like one who has the character of an apostle and will witness what the apostles witness.

D. In John 21:2, he is described as being with the apostles.

E. As discussed above, Bartholomew is not a proper name, but a family surname.

The only information we can gain about the personality and actions of Nathanael come from John 1:45-51. MacArthur notes four lessons from this apostle.

I. His Love of Scripture - John 1:45
   A. Notice how Philip told Nathanael about the Messiah. He didn't say I have found someone to give you a better life. He didn't say, "He will make your marriage better" or "This is the way to true happiness." He pointed out that this was the Messiah the Scriptures had spoken about.

B. Philip and Nathanael's instinct to go to Scripture indicates how they were students of the Old Testament. They were spiritual men. They knew the Scriptures and likely studied them together. They probably had travelled to this area to hear John the Baptist preach.

C. They were truth seekers. They knew the Prophets, so they could recognize Jesus. They did recognize him and followed him for the rest of their lives.

D. There must have been a real surprise in the voice of Philip and in the face of Nathanael when he heard about Jesus being from Nazareth and the son of Joseph, a carpenter.

II. His Prejudice - John 1:46

A. Nathanael apparently had some strong prejudices toward the people of Nazareth. Though he was from a neighboring city that was less prominent than Nazareth, he still looked down on Nazareth it seems.

B. How do you interpret the statement in verse 46, "Can anything good come out of Nazareth?"

1. It could have been a statement of the commonness of Nazareth.

2. It might of been a reference to the thought that the Messiah is not thought of as coming from Nazareth in the Scriptures.

3. It could be that since he lived in the area, it all seems so common and ordinary, he can't imagine the Messiah coming from the city he

visited often just down the road, a son of a carpenter.

4. It could have been a statement of prejudice as MacArthur argues.

C. Nazareth was on one of the main routes going north and south between Jerusalem and Lebanon. It was known as a rough town. It's culture was largely unrefined and uneducated. Not a particularly picturesque place. It is said that the Judaeans looked down on Galilee and even the Galileans looked down on the Nazarenes. Nathanael was echoing the thoughts of the area.

D. Jesus himself had difficulty reaching his hometown (Luke 4:22-29).

E. Prejudice skewed their view and most of the Jews view toward Jesus. Prejudice often blinds the human heart from seeing the truth. It can close one's eyes to the salvation of the gospels (John 1:11; ch. 9; 2 Cor. 4:3-4)

F. His prejudice caused him at first to be skeptical, but it did not keep him from being open to investigating the Messiah. Maybe the influence of a trusted friend in Philip and Philip's invitation to "Come and see" was enough to overcome his initial skepticism.

III. His Sincerity of Heart - John 1:47

A. Jesus, who was the master at reading the character of men (John 2:25), pays Nathanael an incredible compliment.

B. Nathanael was one who is pure-hearted and sincere. He was not a hypocrite. "Though his mind was tainted with some prejudice, his heart was not poisoned by deceit" (p. 142). He was a true Israelite. He was authentic. At a time when many were Israelites in ethnic race and culture, Nathanael was one in his spiritual fervor and actions (Rom. 9:6-7, 2:28-29). He was such a man because he abided in the word (John 8:31-32).

C. He is not going to be guilty as the Pharisees and Scribes were guilty of hypocrisy (Mat. 23:13-33). He was righteous man. A man pure in heart (Mat. 5:8).

D. Are you and I sincere and without deceit in our Christianity?

IV. His Eager Faith - John 1:48-51

  A. Jesus shares with him that He had seen him under the fig tree before Philip had called him.

    1. MacArthur suggests that the fig tree was a common tree planted beside many homes in Israel. That it was often a place to go outside for some privacy and personal meditation. He supposes that Jesus is suggesting he has seen him out under the tree praying and studying. He suggests, "It was not only that Jesus saw his location, but that He saw his heart as well" (p. 145).

    2. Personally, I had always pictured him under a fig tree before Philip had gone to him and

Jesus is saying I saw you even before Philip had called you. Jesus is sharing His omniscient knowledge with Nathanael.

B. Nathanael was impressed by Jesus' statement. He eagerly casts his hope and faith in Jesus as the "Son of God, the King of Israel" (1:49).

C. Jesus says that he will see greater things and then refers to Jacob's vision of the ladder in Genesis 28:11-14.

    1. The meaning of this is somewhat unclear. It seems that Jesus is simply saying you will see amazing things. A chief part of this is the idea that Jesus is the ladder that connects heaven and earth.

    2. He will see the angels confirming Christ as God's son and the marvelous working forth of God's plan.

This is all that we know of Nathanael from Holy Scripture. Tradition suggests he ministered in Persia and India and took the gospel as far as Armenia. We are not sure of how he died. One tradition says he was tied up in a sack and cast into the sea while another claims he was crucified. He was likely a martyr for the faith of Christ.

Matthew

We are familiar with Matthew because of his gospel, but we really don't know much about him personally. Matthew is called Levi the son of Alphaeus (Mark 2:14, Luke 5:27-29). He was a Jewish man who was given a reverential name in Levi. He was likely the brother to James the less as they were both sons of Alphaeus (Matt 10:3, Mark 3:18, Luke 6:15). Yet in all three of the lists of the apostles he is called Matthew. Some suppose that this was a given name after he became a Christian.

Matthew was from Capernaum and is known for his occupation of being a tax collector. Tax collectors are also called publicans in the Scripture. It is thought that he was a customs officer in Capernaum, the area ruled by Herod Antipas. He likely would of had some education. He probably knew Aramaic, Greek, and Latin languages.

MacArthur believes that he was a "Mokhes" tax collector. They had the responsibility of collecting duty on imports and exports, goods for domestic trade, and virtually anything that moved by road. They taxed many other items that were transported. Their assessments were often arbitrary and capricious. There were "Great Mokhes" and "Little Mokhes." Matthew was likely a "Little Mokhes" who was serving at an office. He dealt with people face-to-face.

Tax collectors were some of the most despised people in Jewish society. Matthew must have had strong materialistic desires to pursue and accept such a profession as a tax collector. They were deemed on the same social level as harlots. They were siding with the hated oppressor Rome and their soldiers. They were known for strong-arming money from the people. They were greedy and extorted the people for personal gain. Matthew was likely the most notorious sinner of the apostolic group in his past life.

Three tax collectors are specifically mentioned in the gospels. Each one of them found forgiveness. They were Zaccheus (Luke 19:2-10), the Publican (Luke 18:10-14) and Matthew. They readily came to hear Jesus in Luke 15:1. Jesus mentions that they repented at the preaching of John the Baptist (Luke 7:29). Jesus would admonish the hypocritical religious elite by referring to them in Matthew 21:31-32.

I. Examining Matthew's Call   Matthew 9:9, Luke 5:27-28
   A. This call comes out of nowhere. There must have been some previous communication or experiences between Jesus and Matthew, but we are not aware of them.
   B. No self-respecting Jew in his right might would choose to be a tax collector, unless they were

interested in material gain. It involves effectively cutting yourself off from your own people. MacArthur writes, "After all, since he was banned from the synagogue and forbidden to sacrifice and worship in the temple, he was in essence worse off religiously than a Gentile" (p. 155).

C. His choice to leave the office and follow Jesus was likely an irreversible one. It involved a total change in focus and allegiance. There was likely plenty of people who would take his position. Matthew would never go back and he never regretted it.

D. You wonder if Matthew, who as we will notice later knew the Old Testament well, battled guilt and tender conscience for years as he served as a tax collector. It is almost like Jesus gives him the reason and the motivation to leave this life he knew was not right.

E. Matthew is a great example of conversion to Christ. Do we neglect to appreciate the term "conversion" today?

F. What is so powerful in Jesus' statement, "Follow me"?

II. Having a Feast for Jesus   Matthew 9:10-13, Luke 5:29-32

A. "His first impulse after following Jesus was to bring his closest friends and fellow tax collectors and introduce them to the Savior. He was so thrilled to have found the Messiah that he wanted to introduce Jesus to everyone he knew. He held a large banquet in Jesus' honor and invited them all" (MacArthur 152).

B. Why did Matthew invite these "lowlife sinners?" Luke 5:29-32

C. Was Jesus saying the religious elite did not need a Savior?

  1. No, but there was nothing he could do for them as long as they were self-righteous and self-deceived.

  2. Which group are you and I in this Bible class more closely like? What lesson should we take from this for our own lives?

D. How should we call sinners to repentance today?

III. Matthew's Gospel

A. This tax collector went on to write one of the most popular gospel accounts. There are several things we learn from his gospel that teach us about Matthew.

B. MacArthur writes, "his Gospel quotes the Old Testament ninety-nine times. That is more times than Mark, Luke, and John combined" (p. 156). MacArthur suggests he must have studied the Old Testament on his own in a quest to fill the spiritual void in his life.

C. ESV Study Bible on Matthew's Gospel (p. 1816-1817):

  1. Theme - "This is the story of Jesus of Nazareth, recorded by the apostle Matthew

as a compelling witness that Jesus is the long-anticipated Messiah, who brought the kingdom of God to earth and is the prophesied fulfillment of God's promise of true peace and deliverance for both Jew and Gentile."

   a) Some of the key themes:

      (1) *Portrait of Jesus.* Jesus is the true Messiah, Immanuel, Son of God, King of Israel, and Lord of the church.

      (2) *The bridge between the Old and New Testament.*

      (3) *The new community of faith.* The early church included both Jewish and Gentile Christians, Matthew's gospel would have encouraged them to transcend ethnic and cultural barriers to find unity in service to Jesus the Messiah as members of his universal church.

      (4) *The church is built and maintained by Jesus' continuing presence.*

      (5) *A "great commission" for evangelism and mission.* (Mat. 28:19-20)

      (6) *Jesus' five discourses recorded in Matthew can be viewed as a manual on discipleship.* (Mat. 5-7; 10; 13; 18-20; 24-25)

Though we know only a few details of Matthew's life, we are left with a picture of a man who loved scripture, the lost, and Jesus. He is a great example of repentance and conversion.   He shows the difference Christ's simple petition, "Follow me" can make in the life of a sinner.

Thomas

Thomas was also known as Didymus meaning "twin" (John 11:16). We do not know who his twin sibling might have been. He was a native of Galilee and a fisherman by trade (John 20:24, 21:2).

Thomas appears in all the lists of the apostles (Mat. 10:3, Mark 3:18, Luke 6:15). We do not know how he was called to be an apostle. He is associated with Matthew in Matthew's list (Mat. 10:3).

All of what we know about Thomas as an individual is found through the gospel of John.

Thomas has gained the title in Christianity of "Doubting Thomas." This comes from the story of him desiring to see the risen Christ and touch his wounds with his hands.

John MacArthur writes, "It is probably fair, however, to say that Thomas was a somewhat negative person. He was a worrywart. He was a brooder. He tended to be anxious and angst-ridden. He was like Eeyore in Winnie the Pooh. He anticipated the worst all the time. Pessimism, rather than doubt, seems to have been his besetting sin" (p. 157).

Let us examine the passages that speak of Thomas in John's gospel and see what we think of

Thomas. Do we see him as doubting, pessimistic, realistic, or courageous? What lessons can we draw from his life?

I. Thomas during the Death of Lazarus - John 11:16
   A. Lazarus was sick in Bethany near Jerusalem. Jesus had recently left Jerusalem area because His life was in jeopardy (John 10:39-42). They were doing a very productive work in the wilderness area. Jesus had a close relationship with Lazarus' family.
   B. Jesus desired to use this sickness and death for the glory of God (John 11:4). He knew what He was going to do, thus He tarried two days longer.
   C. Jesus explains to His disciples that Lazarus has died and that He is glad so that they and others might believe.
   D. Thomas will then make his statement to the other disciples when he sees that Jesus is determined to go to Bethany. Thomas says, "Let us also go, that we may die with him" (John 11:16).
      1. How do you interpret his statement?
      2. Is this pessimistic or a faith-filled statement?
      3. Thomas seems committed and desires to be with Jesus. He is going with Jesus even if it means death. You have to admire his courage and commitment.

II. Thomas' Question to Jesus - John 14:5

A. In John 14, Jesus is dear his death and is giving the disciples some final instructions. Jesus is speaking about going away and preparing a place for them.   Thomas is concerned.

B. Thomas says, "Lord, we do not know where you are going.   How can we know the way" (John 14:5).

   1. Thomas speaks the truth and fear of his heart. He loved Jesus and could not bear the thought of being separated from him.   He wants to be where Jesus is.

   2. What if Thomas had not of asked this question? Would we have one of the greatest statements in Scripture (John 14:6)?

   3. How do you view his question?

III. Thomas' Desire for Proof - John 20:24-29

A. Thomas' worse fears do come about and Jesus dies. We don't know where Thomas was during the first few resurrection appearances.   Maybe he was distraught and discouraged. He might have returned to family or work in Galilee.   He missed out on the first Sunday night appearance to the disciples.

B. When he heard the message of the disciples he replied to them, "Unless I see in his hands the mark of the nails, and place my finger into the mark of the nails, and place my hand into his side, I will never believe" (John 20:25)."

1. How do you think this statement was said and meant?
2. What does it reveal about the personality and character of Thomas?
3. Is it wrong to ask and desire proof?

C. The following Sunday night, the disciples were together again with Thomas. Jesus entered into their presence. He invited Thomas to put his finger and hand into his wounds (John 20:26-27).
1. This gives us a description of Jesus' resurrected body.
2. Does Thomas do this act?

D. Thomas, in possibly the greatest statement made by any apostle says, "My Lord and My God."
1. Once he had proof, he believed emphatically.
2. Jesus promises a blessing to all future believers who trust without seeing the resurrection.
3. This confession is the climax of the gospel of John. This is a personal example of the conclusion that John hopes all of his readers will reach (John 20:20-21).

What do you think of Thomas?

How are we like Thomas?

What lessons can we gain from him?

Tradition suggests that Thomas carried the gospel as far as India.   He is said to have been buried in Chennai (Madras), India.   The strongest tradition says that he was martyred for his faith by being run through with a spear.

James the Less, Simon the Zealot, and Judas (not Iscariot)

The final grouping of four apostles includes three seldom mentioned men along with Judas Iscariot who betrays Jesus. These men are going to remain in relative obscurity for Christian history.

Yet, we must keep in mind that these men still are apostles and should be credited with the remarks made about the apostolic group. They left all and followed Jesus (Luke 18:28). They are going to be transformed from common, ordinary men who struggled with doubt to valiant and courageous soldiers who suffer martyrdom for the faith (Eph. 2:20, 1 Cor. 4: 8-13). They are going to hear and carry out the great commission. They are going to be committed and faithful to Jesus.

James, Son of Alphaeus

James is the ninth name on Luke's list of the apostles (Luke 6:14-16). We only know his name, as Scripture records nothing else about him as an individual. Even church history does not record any significant story or record of James. He even had a common name.

Several men are named James in the New Testament. There is James the son of Zebedee and James the half-brother of Jesus who wrote the epistle of James.   James the son of Mary and Joseph became a prominent leader in the early church (Acts 15:13-21, Gal. 1:19, book of James).

The James of our study is described as the son of Alphaeus (Mat. 10:3, Mark 3:18, Luke 6:15, Acts 1:13).   He would have been the brother to Matthew (Mark 2:14).   In Mark 15:40, we learn that James' mother was named Mary.   Matthew 27:56 and Mark 15:47 mention another one of her sons as Joses, an apparent well-known follower of the Lord. His mother was one of the women who came to the tomb of Jesus (Mark 16:1).   When you compare Mark 15:40 and John 19:25.   It is possible that Mary the mother of James the Less and Mary the wife of Clopas are the same person.   This would be assuming that Clopas is another name for Alphaeus or that she remarried.   This would also mean that Mary was the sister to Mary the mother of Jesus and would make Jesus and James the Less and Matthew cousins.

James is thought to be from the Galilee region based on the family associations discussed above. He is also called James the Less in Mark 15:40. This term in greek is *mikros* and literally means "little" and has a primary meaning of "small in stature" (MacArthur p. 171). This could refer to his small physical stature or it could refer to his age in the family or the apostolic group. If not originally, it certainly came also to stand for his influence and prominence. He is certainly "less" in this regard to James the son of Zebedee.

He lived in the shadow of many other great men, yet he did what he could for the Lord. The kingdom needs followers as well as leaders. We should be willing to be in the background serving. Accounts have him taking the gospel to Syria and Persia. Accounts of his death differ, though all record him as a martyr.

Simon the Zealot

Simon is like James in that nothing more is known of him than what is said in the listings of the apostles. His name is mentioned four times and all in the list of the apostles. Luke 6:15 describes him as "Simon called the Zealot" and Matthew 10:4 and Mark 3:18 as "Simon the Cananite." The term Cananite is not a geographical reference, but rather is a reference to political party the Zealots. The term means "to be zealous." The Zealots were a radical faction of Judiasm that opposed Rome and felt compelled to seek to overthrow their political rule. They were devoted to God and country. They were hoping the Messiah would return and lead them to the overthrow of Rome and the re-establishment of the kingdom of Israel. They were often violent in their protest and actions. They would often assassinate Roman soldiers, political leaders, and anyone opposing them. Some even think that the sacking of

Jerusalem by Titus in A.D. 70 was precipitated by the actions of the Zealots.

Simon is listed right before Judas Iscariot in Matthew and Mark which may indicate they were often paired together. It is possible that Judas had strong political intentions and desires as well. It is also interesting to consider Simon and his relationship with Matthew who was a Roman tax collector.

It seems we must be careful about drawing too many conclusions about Simon based on his party affiliation, but it is important to note that Christ is going to change his focus from an earthly kingdom to a spiritual kingdom. From the overthrow of Rome, to the overthrow of sin in the heart of man.

Judas, Not Iscariot

This was probably the most common name in the first century Jewish world and means "Jehovah leads." Yet because of the treachery of Judas Iscariot it is going to have bad associations. Thus John in his gospel must qualify when mentioning this Judas; it is "not Iscariot" (John 14:22). He is also known as Lebbaeus, whose surname was Thaddaeus" (Matt. 10:3). Judas was probably his birth name and the others were given names because of his personality. Thaddaeus means "breast child" evoking the idea of a nursing baby.

Lebbaeus is similar in form and means literally, "heart child." Both names suggest he had a tender child-like heart. He might have been the youngest of his siblings or had an especially close relationship to his mother.

He does ask one recorded question of Jesus in John 14:22. It is not bold or brash, but a simple tender-hearted question. Jesus gives him a wonderful answer sharing the truth that He is open to anyone who would love Him and obey His word. It is possible that Judas was thinking of the political, earthly realm, but Jesus redirected his thoughts to the reigning of Christ within the hearts of individuals.

He is thought to have carried the gospel north and into present day Turkey. He is thought to have been clubbed to death.

Judas Iscariot

Judas is the most notorious and universally scorned of all the apostles. He offers us the most confusion as well. How could a man be in the presence of Jesus for years, witnessing his miracles and teaching, and still betray him for 30 pieces of silver?

Because of our confusion, it is easy to get into speculation surrounding Judas' person and actions. Yet, we must be careful to stay with what the text tells us about Judas and the lessons we are to learn from his life.

Judas' name appears last in all of the lists of the apostles, with the exception of Acts 1 where is name is not listed. Every time his name is mentioned in Scripture we also find a notation about him being the traitor. His name was an extremely common one of the first century. It is a form of Judah and means "Jehovah leads." This name is ironic in that he will be clearly lead by Satan. His surname was Iscariot and signifies the region which he came from. It is derived from the Hebrew term *ish* ("man") and the name of a town, Kerioth. This was probably a town in the south of Judea. He was apparently the only apostle not from the Galilee region. He may have thought of himself as an outsider (MacArthur (p. 182-3). His father was named Simon (John 6:71).

I. His Heart of Unbelief

   A. One of the great paradoxes of biblical truth and difficulties for us to understand is how God's sovereignty works in accordance with man's freedom of choice. We see this tension clearly in the life of Judas. Judas had freedom of choice and Jesus made repeated attempts to get him to repent. Yet, God and Christ knew from the beginning that he would betray him.

   B. Notice these verses about Judas from the lips of Christ.

      1. John 6:64, 70-71

      2. Mat. 26:23-24

      3. John 17:12

   C. The betrayal of Jesus by Judas was prophesied long before Judas was born.

      1. Psalm 41:9 -- John 13:18

      2. Psalm 55:12-14

      3. Zechariah 11:12-13 - Matthew 27:9-10

   D. Jesus chose Judas knowing his heart and intentions, yet Judas acted out of his own free-will.

      1. Luke 22:22 - Jesus affirms both truths in this statement.

      2. Why did Jesus select him to be an apostle?

II. His Motive

   A. There has been much speculation that Judas' motive was one of power. MacArthur wrote: "Judas was not attracted to Christ on a spiritual level. He followed Jesus out of a desire for selfish gain,worldly ambition, avarice, and greed. He sensed Jesus' power and he wanted power like that for himself. . . . Wealth, power, and prestige were what fueled his ambitions" (p. 184).

B. It is very likely in my judgment that Judas had Jewish national hopes and expectations. He was thinking and expecting Jesus to be the King of Israel like David and Solomon. Jesus had the power and popularity to overthrow Rome and lead Israel back to prominence. Some speculate that he grew tired of waiting for Christ to ascend or realized he was focused on different goals, so he betrayed him. It might have even been possible that he was attempting to force the hand of Jesus to ascend to power, which is why he attempts to feign friendship and loyalty in the garden as he kisses Jesus. It is clear that the other apostles and much of the first century Jewish world was looking for a military messiah to lead them. The other apostles slowly grasped Jesus' kingdom's spiritual nature, but Judas apparently never came on board.

C. The Holy Spirit's answer, and thus the only answer that really matters, is that Judas was greedy for wealth and power.

    1. Matthew 26:14-18 - Following the anointing by Mary with costly ointment (Mat. 26:6-13, John 12:1-8) and the resurrection of Lazarus, Judas contacts the chief priests looking to

negotiate his best offer for Jesus. He received 30 pieces of silver.

2. John 12:4-6 - Judas was a thief!

3. Acts 1:16-20 - Peter says he acquired a field with the reward of his wickedness. Peter is making the allusion that he went after the money and it yielded him a "Field of blood."

4. Luke 22:3 and John 13:2 indicates that Satan entered him. The thought is that he turned his heart and life over to the control and influence of Satan.

III. His Actions

A. Judas never embraced the spiritual kingdom of Christ. The worldliness in his heart was never conquered. He kept his focus on the physical, rather than the spiritual.

B. He lived the life of a hypocrite.

1. The other disciples did not know he was the one who would betray Jesus.

2. In the upper room - John 13:21-30

3. In the garden of Gethsemane - Mat 26:47-50, Luke 22:47-48

C. He was overcome with great guilt.

1. "He found himself in a hell of his own making" (MacArthur p. 195).

2. Matthew 27:3-4

a. It seems his remorse was not the same as repentance. He regretted his decision or changed his mind. He was sorry, not in a godly way, but rather in sorrow that his sin had not satisfied him the way he had hoped (2 Cor. 7:9-11, Heb. 12:15-17) His remorse was brought from seeing his sin from a different perspective. He saw his sin in its full horror. All of the hopes and promises he thought it would bring, had not come.

b. His response was to give the money back to the Jewish leaders.

c. He states, "I have sinned by betraying innocent blood." Matthew 27:4.

d. How do you understand his remorse?

e. How difficult is it for those who are bitter, resentful, remorseful, and guilty over their sin to truly repent and turn to the grace of God? Why is it so hard?

D. His Suicide

1. Matthew 27:5 - "He went and hanged himself."

2. Acts 1:16-20 - "Falling headlong he burst open in the middle and all his bowels gushed out."

3. Judas apparently committed suicide by hanging himself. His body was likely left to decay while hanging and eventually fell and burst open on the rocks. It is also possible that he tried to hang himself, but the rope or tree broke and he fell to the rocks and died.

4. Why did he take such action?

a. He was of sound mind it seems, but was overcome with guilt for his sin. His plan had not worked. The materialistic greed had not given him the happiness he thought it would.
b. He must have felt hopeless, having missed out on the essential message of the Gospel. He might have put his hope in a political revolt by Jesus, and when it doesn't happen, he gives up.
c. Possibly Judas felt like an outsider and outcast. He didn't fit with the apostles, especially now, and he didn't fit with the Jewish leaders who had just used him. Loneliness probably was a powerful emotion for him.

IV. Lessons
  A. Some lessons from MacArthur (p. 197-8).
    1. Judas is a tragic example of lost opportunity.
    2. Judas is the epitome of wasted privilege.
    3. Judas is the classic example of how the love of money is the root of all kinds of evil (1 Tim. 6:10).
    4. Judas is proof of the patient, fore-bearing goodness and loving-kindness of Christ.
    5. Judas demonstrates how the sovereign will of God cannot be thwarted by any means. Judas prompted by Satan brought about a seemingly great defeat for Jesus, but it would

lead to His greatest triumph (Heb. 2:14, 1 John 3:8).

6.Judas is a vivid demonstration of the deceitfulness and fruitfulness of hypocrisy. His hypocrisy could not stay hidden. It eventually was exposed.

B. Some additional thoughts:

1. Just like we can see ourselves in the successes and failures of the other apostles, so we can with Judas as well. We are often much more like him than we want to admit.

   a. We can easily hear lesson after lesson with little change in our behavior or heart.

   b. We can be greedy, hypocritical, and lustful of power.

2. Maybe Judas is a part of the apostolic group to show the love Jesus demonstrated for his enemy. Jesus loved him throughout and sought for his repentance.

3. Peter and Judas are a great comparative study. They both will fail miserably around the death of Jesus. Both will feel guilt and remorse. But they will handle it drastically differently. We can follow either example.

Works Cited

Bruce, A.B. **The Training of the Twelve.** Public Domain. Accordance Bible Software

MacArthur, John. **Twelve Ordinary Men: How the Master Shaped His Disciples for Greatness and What He Wants to Do with You.** W Publishing Group: Nashville TN. 2002

Skipper, W.E. **The Twelve** self-published, 1970.